MOUNTIES FOR KIDS

AN RCMP ACTIVITY BOOK

TOM HUNTER

VICTORIA
VANCOUVER
CALGARY

Heritage House Publishing, Ltd.
heritagehouse.ca

Cataloguing information available from Library and Archives Canada

ISBN 978-1-77203-283-3

Edited by Audrey McClellan
Cover and interior design by Darlene Nickull

This book was produced using FSC®-certified, acid-free paper, processed chlorine free and printed with vegetable-based inks.

We acknowledge the financial support of the Government of Canada through the Canada Book Fund (CBF) and the Canada Council for the Arts, and the Province of British Columbia through the British Columbia Arts Council and the Book Publishing Tax Credit.

22 21 20 19 2 3 4 5

Printed in Canada

Canada's first Prime Minister suggested that Canada should have a police force capable of maintaining law and order in the West. On May 23, 1873, his recommendation was given Royal Assent. On August 30 that year the North-West Mounted Police became a reality. To find this Prime Minister's name, trace the line from letter to letter, spelling as you go.

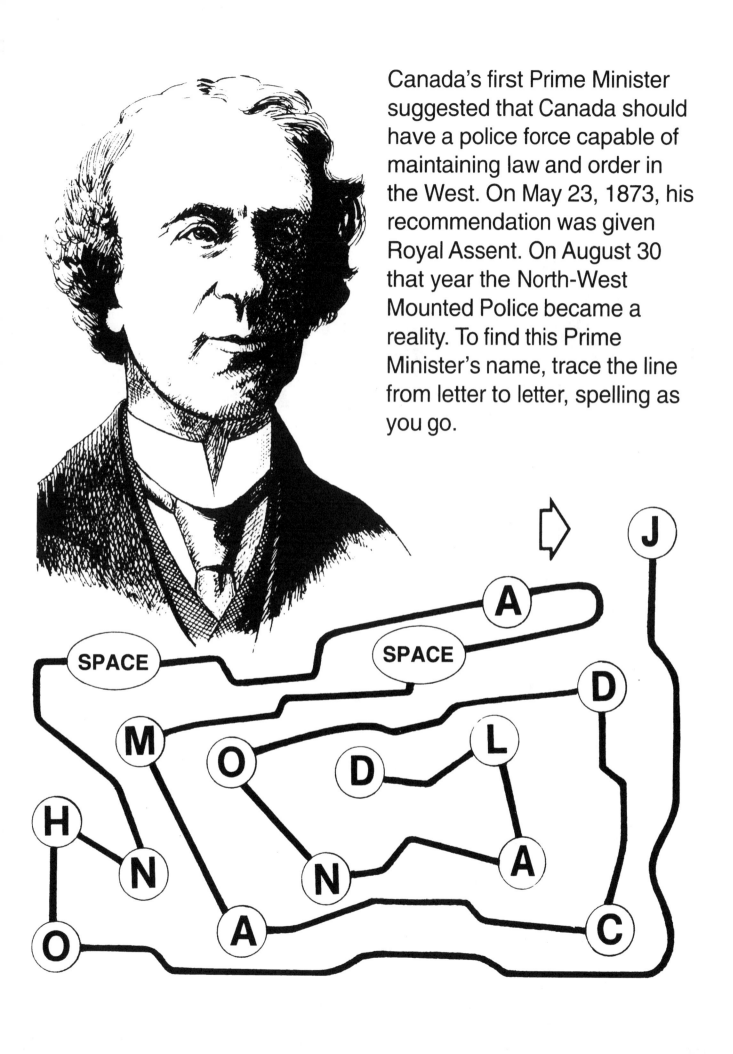

The first North-West Mounted Police saddles were the same kind used by the British army. See how many words you can make from the letters in the word "saddle." Twelve is a good score.

SADDLE

_____

_____

_____

_____

_____

_____

_____

_____

_____

_____

Answers: Add, saddle, ale, as, dad, dale, dead, deal, lea, led, sad, sale, seal, sled.

The highest-ranking officer in the force is the Commissioner. In 1873 the man pictured here became the first permanent Commissioner To learn his name, fill in the blank above each of the letters below with the letter that comes after it in the alphabet.

_ _ _ _ _ _ _   _ _ _ _ _ _

F D N Q F D   E Q D M B G

Answer: George French

On July 8, 1874, the Mounties began their famous 1,300-kilometre march west. En route they saw great herds of buffalo. Assistant Commissioner James Macleod was so impressed by the great beasts that he suggested using their image on the North-West Mounted Police cap badges and buttons. If you carefully fill in all the shapes with odd numbers, you will see one of these imposing animals.

While patrolling the West, the Mounties came in contact with many Indigenous peoples. The names of nine of them are hidden in the square below. Search for them across or down.

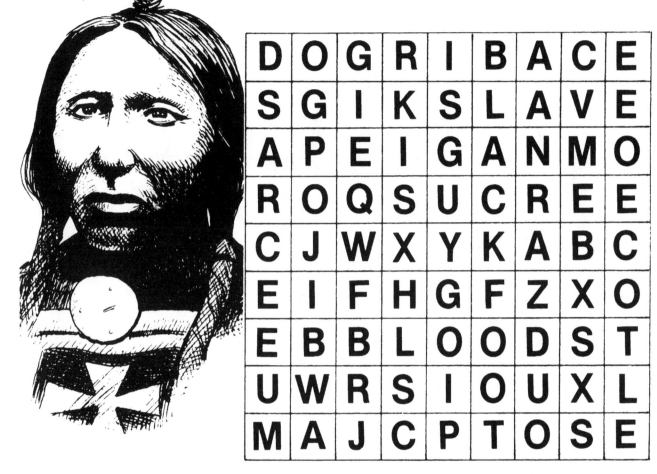

D	O	G	R	I	B	A	C	E
S	G	I	K	S	L	A	V	E
A	P	E	I	G	A	N	M	O
R	O	Q	S	U	C	R	E	E
C	J	W	X	Y	K	A	B	C
E	I	F	H	G	F	Z	X	O
E	B	B	L	O	O	D	S	T
U	W	R	S	I	O	U	X	L
M	A	J	C	P	T	O	S	E

Answers: Blackfoot, Blood, Cree, Dogrib, Ojibwa, Piegan, Sarcee, Sioux, Slave.

DID YOU KNOW?

Indigenous people from various tribes were hired as scouts in the early days of the North-West Mounted Police.

The most famous and experienced of the scouts hired by the North-West Mounted Police was the son of a Blood Nation woman and a Scottish trader.

To find this scout's name, trace along the line, spelling as you go.

Start here: ➡

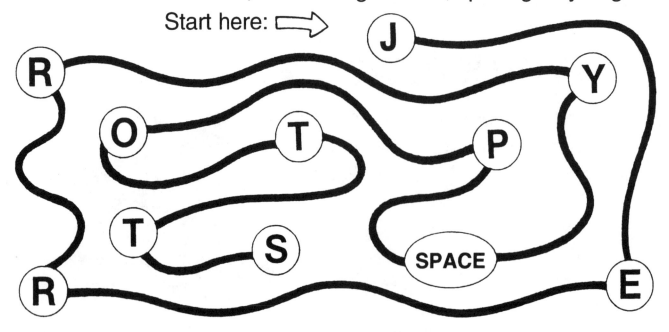

Here are two pictures of a North-West Mounted Police Inspector of 1888. Try to find six things that are different in picture two.

Answers:

In 1883 the general manager of the Canadian Pacific Railway commended the North-West Mounted Police for its work in maintaining law and order during the building of the cross-Canada railway. You can find out that general manager's name by starting at the letter "W" and reading every second letter. Go around twice.

Answer: William Van Horne.

Which of the pieces below will complete
this jigsaw puzzle of a pony?

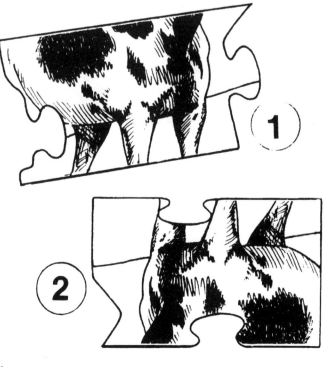

Answer: Number three.

Which two of these six North-West Mounted Police constables are identical?

Answer: Constables two and five.

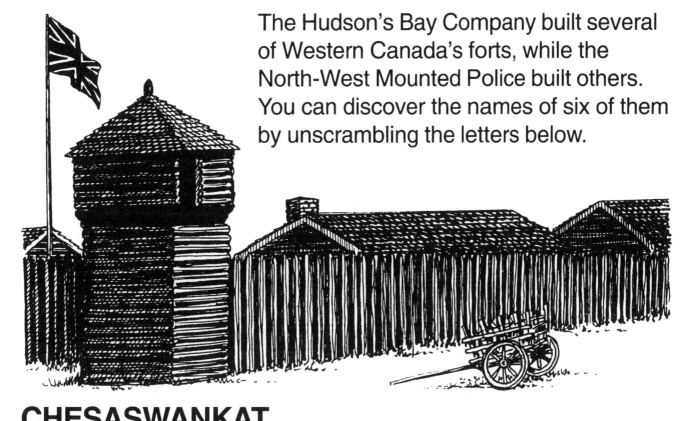

The Hudson's Bay Company built several of Western Canada's forts, while the North-West Mounted Police built others. You can discover the names of six of them by unscrambling the letters below.

CHESASWANKAT _____

RYGALCA _____

NOTRACL _____

LEEEST _____

SHAWL _____

TIPT _____

Answers:

1. Saskatchewan (NWMP). 2. Calgary (NWMP) 3. Carlton (HBC). 4. Steele (NWMP).
5. Walsh (NWMP). 6. Pitt (HBC).

DID YOU KNOW?

The third son of the famous author Charles Dickens was a Sub-Inspector in the North-West Mounted Police stationed at Fort Pitt.

This dignified Cree leader figured prominently in the North-West Rebellion. He was highly respected by many Indigenous tribes and the North-West Mounted Police. To learn his name, start at the "C" and read every second letter. Go around twice.

The Adams revolver was the first side arm issued to the North-West Mounted Police. Next came the Enfield revolver. Both of these weapons proved unsatisfactory and were followed by a succession of more suitable revolvers. How many words can you make from the letters in the word "revolvers"? Twenty would be an excellent score.

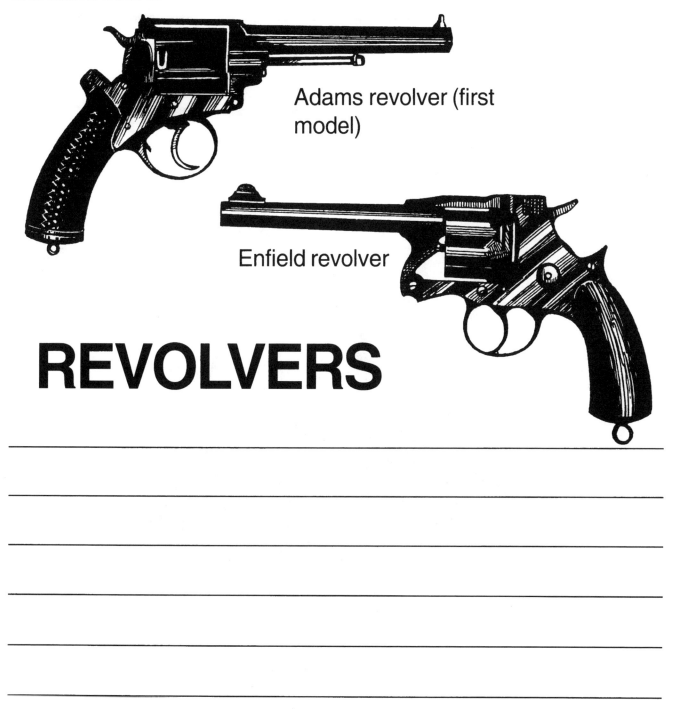

Adams revolver (first model)

Enfield revolver

REVOLVERS

_____

_____

_____

_____

_____

This famous Mountie was involved in the Riel and North-West Rebellions. He was responsible for maintaining law and order during the building of the Canadian Pacific Railway, Sitting Bull's stay in Canada, and the Yukon gold rush. To find his name, start at the arrow and follow along the line, spelling as you go.

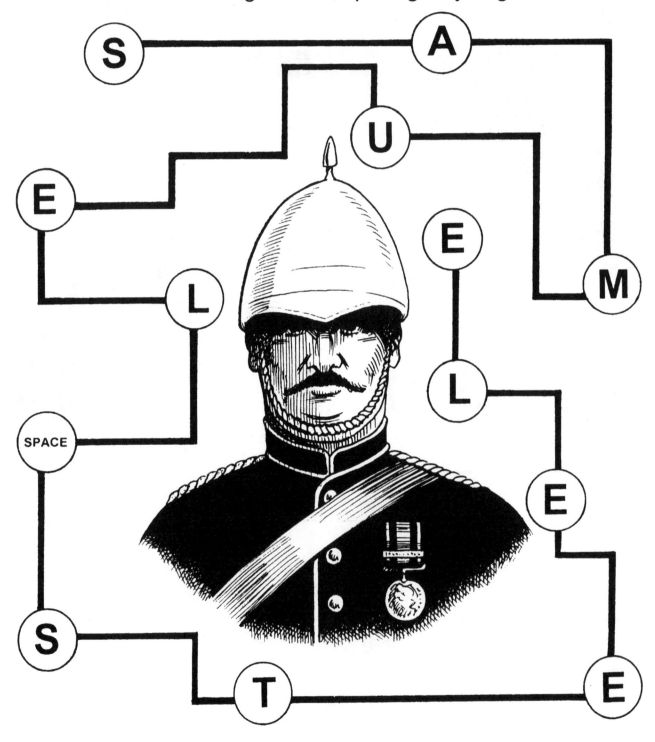

Which of the flags below flew over the NWMP post at the top of the Chilkoot Pass during the Yukon gold rush of 1898?

Answer: Flag number two, the Union Jack.

Since the beginning of the force, its members have used many types of transportation. The names of nine are hidden in the letters below. Look for them down and across.

X	A	Y	B	C	D	E	H	Z
F	G	I	K	L	N	O	M	J
L	A	G	S	T	W	P	X	T
S	N	O	W	S	H	O	E	S
C	A	D	O	G	S	L	E	D
A	B	C	H	O	C	K	L	A
N	O	T	O	R	A	W	T	M
O	A	I	R	C	R	A	F	T
E	T	O	S	K	I	D	O	O
S	E	N	E	T	A	G	I	F
S	E	W	A	G	O	N	F	R
E	G	J	M	O	F	H	I	N

Answers: Aircraft, boat, canoe, car, dogsled, horse, skidoo, snowshoes, wagon.

DID YOU KNOW?

A Mounted Policeman's pay was once as low as 40 cents per day.

In 1920 the Royal North-West Mounted Police became the Royal Canadian Mounted Police. Over the years the RCMP has absorbed several other Canadian police forces. The first was a federal force that provided protection for government buildings in Ottawa and bodyguards for various government leaders. To learn the name of this force, fill in the blank above each letter with the letter that comes after it in the alphabet.

— — — — — — — — — — — — — —

C N L H M H N M   O N K H B D

In the winter of 1931-32, despite temperatures of –40 degrees, the Mounties embarked on a manhunt for the murderer of a young constable. The suspect was Albert Johnson, who came to be known as the Mad Trapper of Rat River. The hunt took 48 days and covered 240 kilometres through the northern Yukon, and for the first time in the history of the RCMP an airplane was called in for assistance. Before the hunt ended, one policeman was killed and two were wounded. When Johnson was eventually shot and killed, he was found to be carrying $2,500 in Canadian and American currency as well as a quantity of gold dust.

See if you can find the Mad Trapper in the snow by filling in all the shapes having odd numbers.

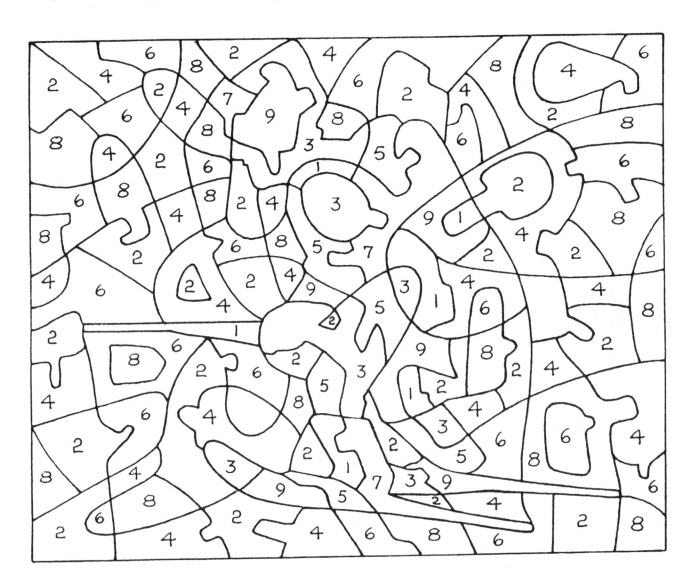

Below are two pictures of a McLaughlin-Buick, the Mounties' first police car. Try to find six things that are different in picture two.

This picture of a Mounted Policeman's horse has been drawn with one continuous line. See if you can find the end of the line.

START HERE

Which shadow belongs to this police dog?

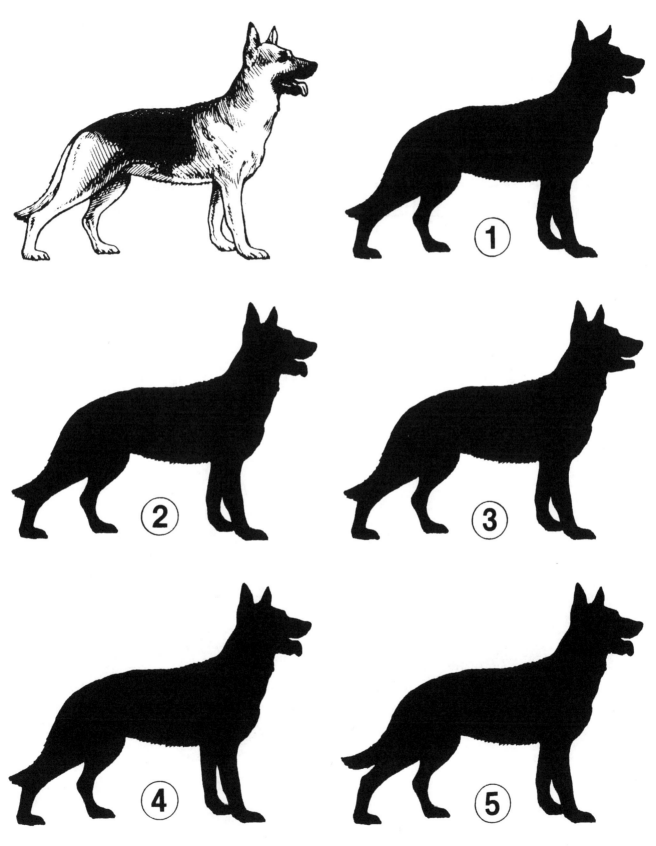

Answer: Shadow number two.

In 1944 the RCMP vessel *St. Roch* became the first in history to navigate Canada's Northwest Passage in both directions. It later became the first ship to sail completely around North America by way of the Panama Canal. The *St. Roch* can now be seen beside the Maritime Museum in Vancouver.

To learn the name of the man who commanded the *St. Roch* and its crew of seven, fill in the blank above each of the letters below with the letter that appears before it in the alphabet.

— — — — —   — — — — — —
I F O S Z   M B S T F O

Draw this Constable by copying one square at a time.

If you can unravel this picture puzzle, you will come up with the name of a world-famous law enforcement agency.

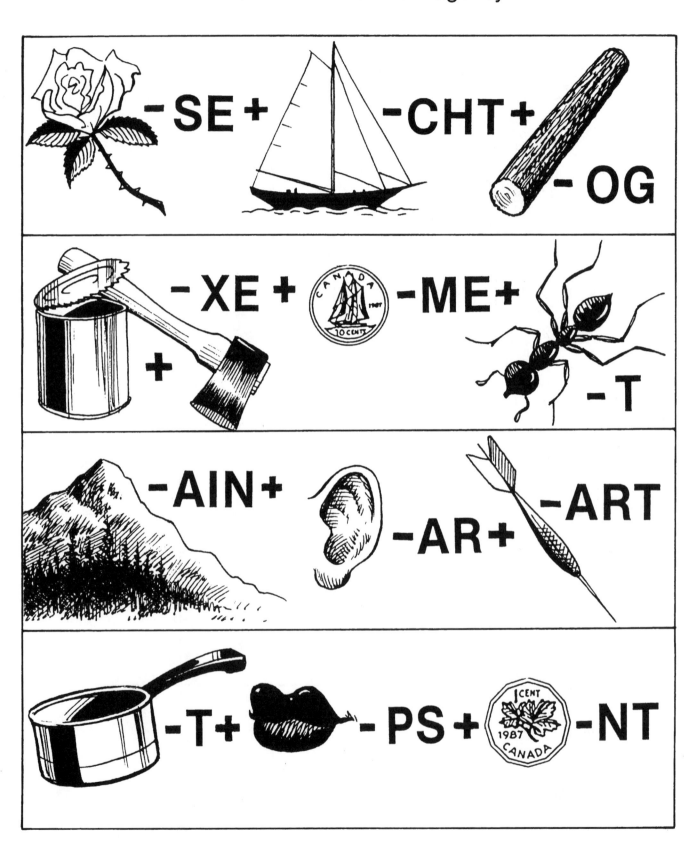

The famous RCMP musical ride has performed all over the world. Which of these horses and their riders are identical?

Answer: Horse and rider numbers six and two.

Try your hand at drawing the other half of this Mountie.

The RCMP aviation section was brought into service
in 1937 with the purchase of four aircraft from the
de Havilland Aircraft Company.

To find out what these aircraft were called, trace along the line,
spelling as you go.   Start here.

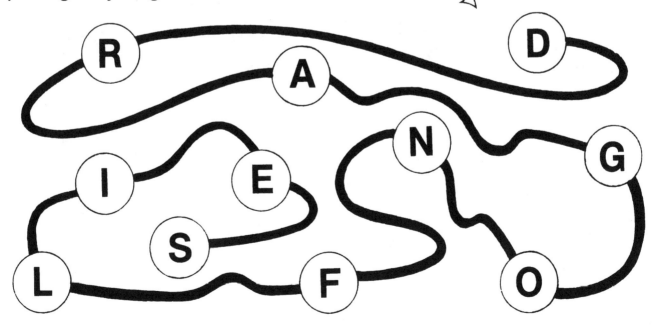

Terrorists have stolen two vans and disguised them as legitimate business vehicles. They are not very good at spelling. Can you help the Mounties find the two stolen vans?

In the West, the RCMP has a stock section that works closely with brand inspectors to help prevent cattle rustling. Cattle brands often depict the name of the ranch or cattle company that owns the cattle. See if you can match these brands with their ranch names.

1		ARROW HEAD
2		TWIN RAFTERS
3		KEYSTONE
4		TEA POT
5		LUCKY P
6		SEVEN UP
7		LAZY R
8		DOUBLE T
9		KEYHOLE
10		ROCKING H

Answers:

1. Lazy R. 2. Rocking H. 3. Keyhole. 4. Seven Up. 5. Keystone. 6. Double T. 7. Lucky P. 8. Twin Rafters. 9. Arrow Head. 10. Teapot.

My partner and I were separated while searching the woods for a fleeing suspect. You can help us get together by filling in all the shapes below with dots in them.

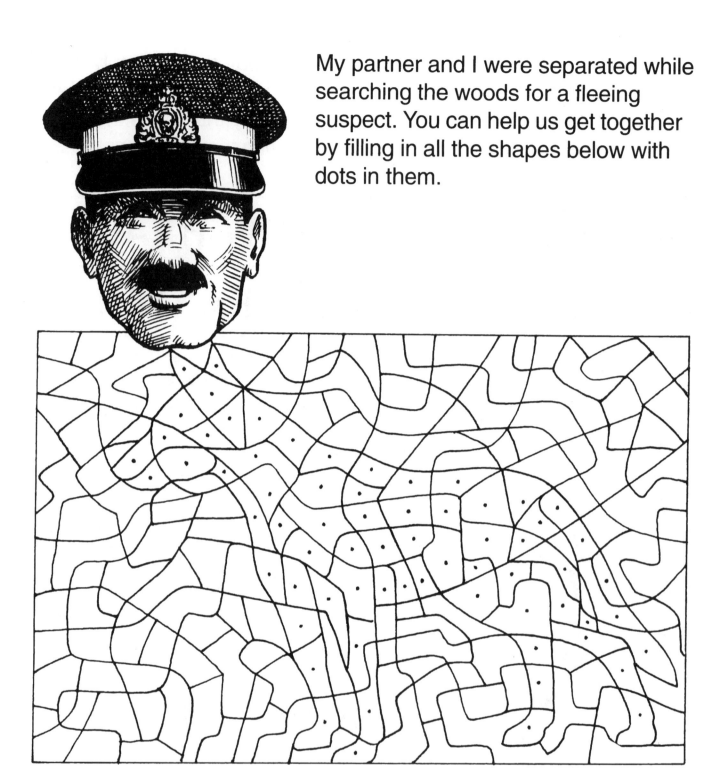

DID YOU KNOW?

In 1935 the RCMP purchased a German shepherd named Dale, the first official canine member of the force.

Which shadow belongs to these handcuffs?

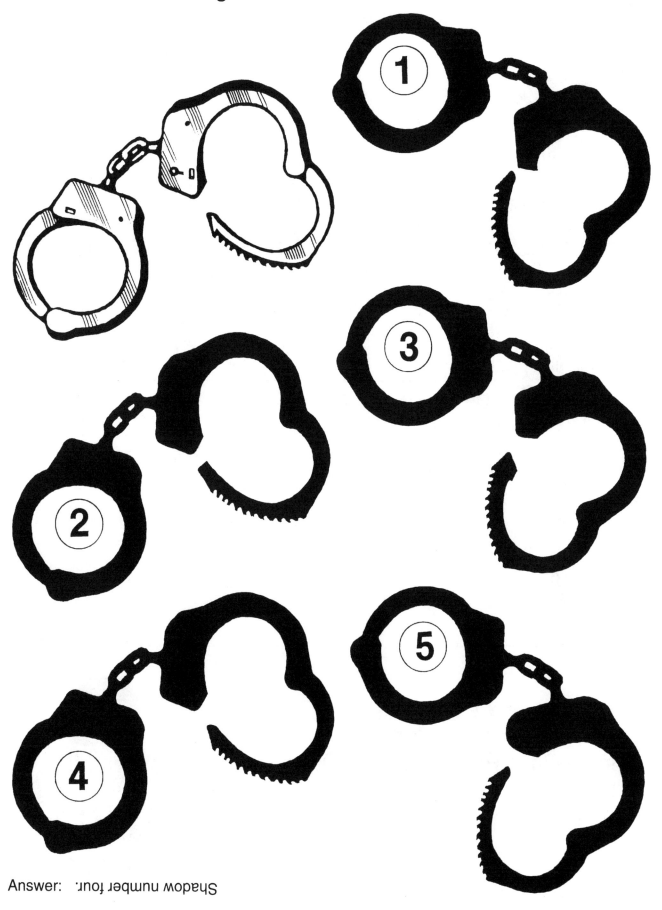

Answer: Shadow number four.

Hidden in the square below are the names of eight instruments in the RCMP band. Search down and across to find them.

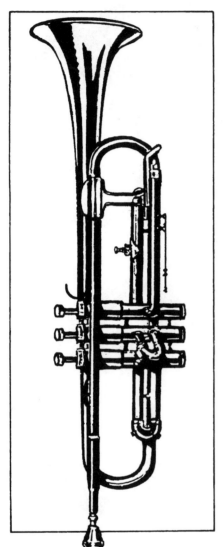

C	A	T	U	B	A	T	B
L	C	R	D	A	E	R	F
A	G	O	H	S	I	U	F
R	J	M	K	S	L	M	L
I	M	B	N	O	O	P	U
N	P	O	B	O	E	E	T
E	Q	N	R	N	S	T	E
T	T	E	D	R	U	M	U

DID YOU KNOW?

In 1948 the RCMP band left Ottawa and began to tour Canada, and later the United States and many parts of the world.

RCMP band emblem

The RCMP's last dog patrol took place in 1969, when one constable and an Indigenous special constable drove two teams 160 kilometres, from Old Crow in the Yukon to Fort McPherson in the Northwest Territories. See how well you can draw the other half of this Siberian husky.

This Beechcraft airplane was one of two purchased by the RCMP in 1946. Picture one differs from picture two in six ways. Can you find the differences?

Below are pictured some of the insignia that may be found on a Mountie's sleeve. To find what these badges denote, unscramble the letters accompanying them

1 FTAFS TNAGERES

2 SMLIAUC IDER

3 MKMAARSN

4 RIA IONSVIDI

5 RESGENAT JORMA

6 RUCTTROINS

7 OGD SAMTRE

8 LARROCOP

Here are three undercover members of the RCMP. From the information below, you should be able to find out which is the sergeant.

The sergeant is to the right of the constable.
The constable is to the left of the corporal.
The sergeant is not in the middle.

Answer: 1. Constable. 2. Corporal. 3. Sergeant.

DID YOU KNOW?

In 1918 the government of Canada sent a Royal North-West Mounted Police cavalry squadron of 6 officers and 184 men to assist in the Allied intervention in the Russian civil war.

Study the licence plates for five minutes, then close the book and write down the numbers and the provinces they belong to.

NEW BRUNSWICK
NB 4133

BRITISH COLUMBIA
BC 280

QUEBEC
QUE 119

SASKATCHEWAN
SAS 213

ONTARIO
ONT 201

ALBERTA
AL 664

PRINCE EDWARD ISLAND
PEI 003

NEWFOUNDLAND
NF 606

MANITOBA
MAN 411

NOVA SCOTIA
NS 508

TRUE OR FALSE

	T	F
1. The RCMP graduated its first female troop from the Regina depot in 1985.	☐	☐
2. The NWMP built Fort Saskatchewan in what is now Alberta.	☐	☐
3. In the original Musical Ride, only white horses were used.	☐	☐
4. The RCMP celebrated its 100th anniversary in 1979.	☐	☐
5. In 1900, Mounted Police cavalry units were sent to South Africa	☐	☐
6. Constable Graburn was the first Mountie killed in the line of duty.	☐	☐

Answers: 1. False. The first female troop graduated in 1974. 2. True. 3. False. No white horses were ever used. 4. False. It was celebrated in 1973. 5. True. 6. True.

One of the Mounties' many duties is the enforcement of our traffic laws. Our roads and highways have many different traffic signs to help us drive safely. Do you know what the signs on this page indicate?

Answers:

This picture of a police dog has been drawn with one continuous line. Trace the line carefully to find its end.

START HERE

Much police work requires writing reports. These reports must be well written, and correct spelling is essential. Underline the word in column A or in column B that you believe is spelled correctly.

VEHICLE	VEHICAL
WITNESS	WITTNES
BURGLERY	BURGLARY
ARRESTED	ARESSTED
INJURIES	INJURYS
IMPARED	IMPAIRED
CONTERBAND	CONTRABAND
ILLEGAL	ILLEAGLE
CONFESSION	CONFFESSION
WHEAPON	WEAPON
ACSIDENT	ACCIDENT
ASSAULT	ASSALT

Which shadow belongs to this RCMP horse?

Answer: Shadow number four.

Can you drive this police car back to the police building without having to stop at more than two traffic lights?

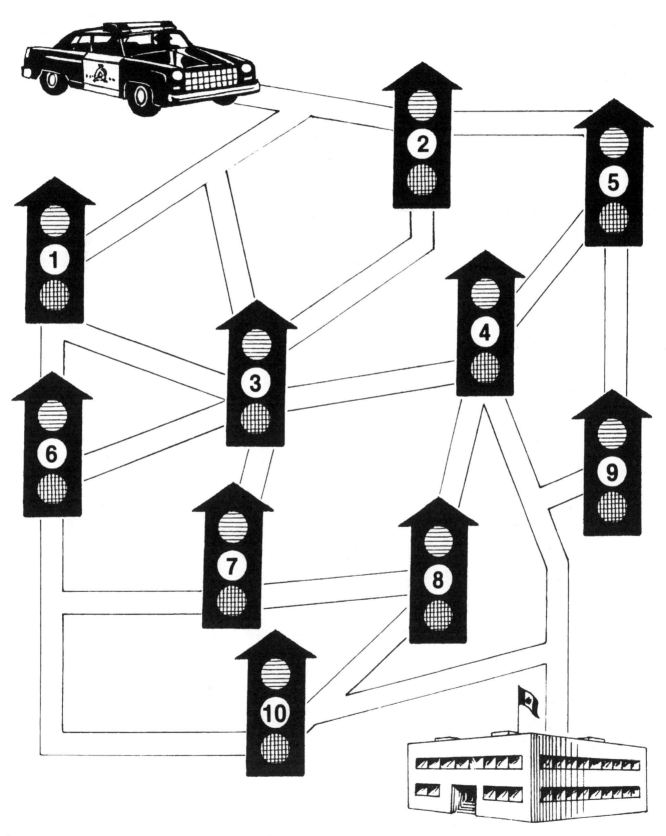

Answer: Follow the roads to traffic lights numbered three and four.

Fingerprints often play an important part in solving crimes. See if you can match the print at right with one of those below.

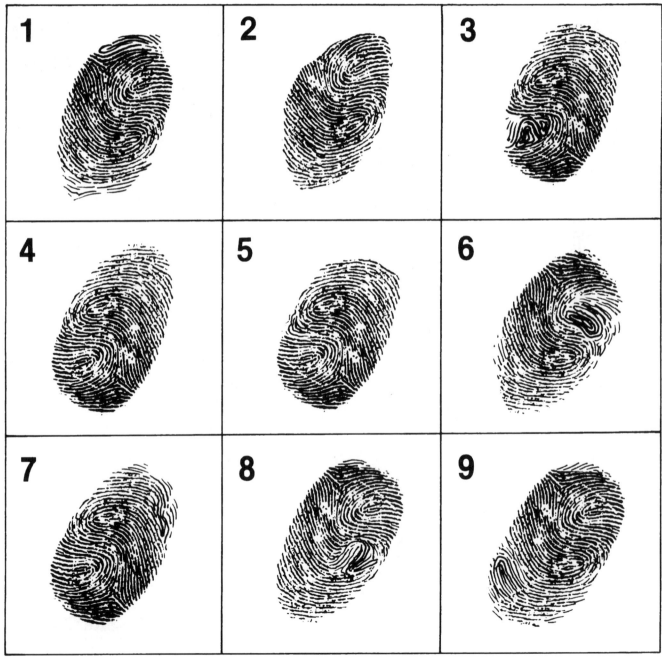

Believe it or not, more than one hundred words can be made from the letters in the word "policewoman!" See how many you can make.

POLICEWOMAN

_____

_____

_____

_____

_____

_____

_____

_____

_____

_____

_____

_____

Have someone time you while you study the clues on this page for one minute. Then close the book and write down the names of all the clues you can remember. Twelve is good, sixteen is excellent!

phone number

match book

watch crystal

CLOVERDALE PIZZA FREE DELIVERY 208-1134

586-4546

fingerprint

pocket knife

key

lipstick

broken glass

bottle top

shell casing

broken comb

cigarette butt

safety pin

screw

gum wrapper

pencil stub